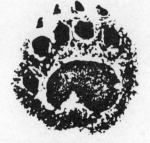

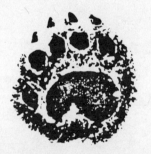

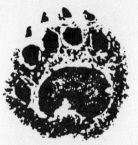

Collection Development Information

5-01	6	8-01
2/06	9-1	4/05
2/2014	17-1	3/2013

The Smokey Bear Story

The Smokey Bear Story

Ellen Earnhardt Morrison

Morielle Press
Alexandria, Virginia

Approved by the Forest Service, United States Department of Agriculture, in cooperation with the National Association of State Foresters and the Advertising Council. (Authorized by 18 U.S.C § 711)

FIRST EDITION

Published by Morielle Press
P. O. Box 10612, Alexandria, Virginia 22310-0612

Manufactured in the United States of America

ISBN: 0-9622537-4-X

Library of Congress Catalog Card Number: 94-73401

Dedicated to
my grandchildren
and all other friends of
Smokey Bear

Contents

Smokey Bear Stays Young 1
Smokey and His Artists 5
The Live Bear 17
Smokey Bear Still Going Strong 23
Smokey Cares About Trees 25
Trash Fires 28
Smokey and the Forest Creatures 29
Smokey and the Cubs 35
When Smokey Was Thirty 38
Smokey Says 40
"The" Bear 45
Sometimes Smokey Is Big 46
A Law to Protect Smokey 49
Children and Smokey 51
Junior Forest Rangers 54
Smokey's Fiftieth Birthday 55
What Does Smokey Stand For? 57
Glossary 58
Index 59
Acknowledgments 60

Smokey Bear Stays Young

Surely you know who Smokey Bear is. You have seen him on posters and on television. You have seen his picture in magazines and newspapers. You may have heard him on the radio. He asks you to help prevent forest fires.

But did you know that Smokey is fifty years old? He celebrated that important birthday in 1994.

When people reach fifty years old, they begin to slow down a bit. It is not the same with Smokey, because he has not slowed down with age. He is just as young and active as ever.

There is a good reason why Smokey does not grow old. He was not born like other bears, but was invented to be an advertising symbol for forest fire prevention. He was full-grown the first time anybody ever saw him.

Smokey Bear's story goes back many years, to a time when the United States was in a big war.

A lot of wood was used in making things needed for fighting the war. That wood came from forests in many parts of the country. It was very important to protect those forests, especially from fire.

Forest fires happen naturally, and nothing can stop that. Yet people cause many fires, by accident or carelessness.

While the war was on, many of the fire fighters were away from home in military service, or working in war factories. That made it very hard for the people at home

In the early 1940's, the United States and other Allied Nations were engaged in World War II against the Axis Powers (Germany, Japan, and Italy). The United States seemed fairly safe from direct attack on its mainland, until one spring day in 1942, when a Japanese submarine surfaced and fired shells on the coast of California. No great damage was done, but it was frightening. What if more attacks came? Enemy shells, or sabotage, could easily set off forest fires that would be a serious threat to vast timber resources, and to the nation's war effort.

to fight the forest fires that broke out. If only the accidental fires could be prevented, it would help a lot.

Then somebody thought about asking people to be careful and not cause fires in the forests. To spread this message a new group was formed, called the Cooperative Forest Fire Prevention (CFFP) Program. They were the ones who first thought of using an animal as a symbol for forest fire prevention. They chose a bear.

August 9, 1944, was Smokey Bear's "birthday," because that was when the fire prevention bear was first described: His fur should be black or brown. His face should be like a panda's, and have a quizzical expression. And he should wear a hat. The first description did not call for the bear to wear pants. The blue jeans were soon added, to give him a work outfit.

Please, Mister, DON'T BE CARELESS

PREVENT FOREST FIRES
Greater danger than ever!

Just before Smokey Bear appeared, Bambi was loaned by the Walt Disney Studios to the Advertising Council for use in the 1944 Fire Prevention Campaign. It was Bambi's popularity that persuaded the CFFP Program to look for an animal symbol of their own.

The Cooperative Forest Fire Prevention (CFFP) Program was created by the U. S. Department of Agriculture (USDA) Forest Service, often called the U. S. Forest Service (USFS). CFFP is a Federal program of the USFS, supported by the State Foresters and the Advertising Council. All three work together to develop fire prevention activities around the country. The CFFP Program plans the advertising, and the Advertising Council's primary role is to sponsor and distribute the advertising to the media. Much other Smokey Bear material is produced and distributed by the USFS and State Foresters.

The Wartime Advertising Council was formed during World War II to prepare and distribute important public service messages for the government, to the people of the United States. The Council was a group of advertising agencies who gave their services free, to aid the war effort. After the war, they continued their volunteer services, as the Advertising Council. Forest Fire Prevention is one of their longest running campaigns, and Smokey Bear is one of the most widely-recognized advertising symbols in the world.

This poster from Canada gives Smokey's message in French.

Smokey and His Artists

After the people of the CFFP Program decided to use a bear as their symbol for forest fire prevention, they had to get a picture of him. So they asked artist Albert Staehle to paint one. He was famous for his animal pictures.

SMOKEY SAYS—

Hold 'til it's cold... prevent forest fires

Staehle read the description they gave him and set to work. Soon he had finished the first picture of the new animal symbol called "Smokey."

Staehle's painting was used in the advertising campaign for 1945.

Smokey Bear was a big success. People in all parts of the United States liked the bear and his idea of forest fire prevention.

Staehle's first poster of Smokey Bear was so popular that he was asked to paint the

Here is Smokey in one of Staehle's posters.

advertising campaign posters for the next two years.

You would hardly recognize Smokey Bear in the first posters. They did not look like he does today.

Staehle pictured Smokey with a smaller hat, a larger head, and a face with very big round eyes. After Staehle, various other artists painted the bear's picture, each in his own way. As a result, Smokey did not always look the same. Yet his friends always recognized him and listened to his message.

Because Smokey Bear is an advertising symbol, each artist has to include certain items, such as the campaign hat and blue jeans. Items added later were the belt and buckle, the name "Smokey" on his hat, and the shovel he sometimes carries. As you know, two students in a classroom can draw the same subject, but their pictures will not look alike. It is just the same with artists. They draw the same character, put everything into the picture that is supposed to be there, but the pictures will always be a little different. That's why the fire prevention bear's appearance has changed from time to time.

The bear looks very different in another early picture of Smokey and friends. In this poster, the term "woods fires" is used instead of "forest fires."

Already busy with forest fire prevention, Smokey Bear puts out
a campfire in Albert Staehle's first poster, 1944.

remember–only you can
PREVENT FOREST FIRES!

The burned forest and the teardrop in this fawn's eye tell the sad story of animals who are displaced by forest fire.

Smokey's friends don't play with matches.

Only <u>you</u> can prevent forest fires.

This is a very busy picture of children enjoying a forest. They know that the words on the poster are very true. Smokey is there, too, at the bottom corner.

Forest friends gather about Smokey Bear for this 1979 poster.
It is similar to the "Remember: there are babes in the woods" poster of 1973.

Smokey's A, B, C's were featured in the 1964 advertising campaign.

We should all be concerned about the future because we will have to spend the rest of our lives there.

— CHARLES F. KETTERING

This is the CFFP Program poster that was used during Smokey Bear's 50th Birthday celebration.

Later artist Rudy Wendelin at the USDA, doing art for the Forest Service, made Smokey Bear the tall, friendly, capable character that we know today. He was the one who first drew the the bear's front paws to look like hands. That made it seem natural for him to do all sorts of interesting activities in the pictures of him.

This is Smokey as he looked in a 1973 picture by Wendelin.

After World War II, Rudy Wendelin returned from duty in the U. S. Navy and went to work for the USDA as a career artist. He soon met the new CFFP advertising bear. With his imagination, wit, and artistic talent, he helped develop the image of Smokey Bear. He was known affectionately in Forest Service circles as "Smokey's artist." He did none of the art for the annual Advertising Council's fire prevention campaign. However, whenever Smokey art was needed at the Forest Service for special events, programs, posters, catalogs, coloring sheets, and such, Wendelin was there. Even the design for the CFFP Program's award, the Smokey Statuette, was created by Wendelin. He was often called the "keeper of Smokey's image." Long after his 1973 retirement from the USDA, he continued to produce Smokey Bear art.

USA 20¢

When a commemorative stamp was planned for Smokey Bear's 40th Birthday in 1984, Rudy Wendelin created the art. He was honored at the "First Day of Issue" ceremony for the stamp in Capitan, New Mexico, on August 13, 1984. The stamp shows the Smokey Bear advertising symbol in the gray background, with the little live bear cub clinging to a burned brown snag in the foreground.

As we have seen, all the pictures of Smokey Bear have not looked alike. But in them all, he has had a confident, friendly manner that made it easy to believe him. Through the work of many artists, year after year, people have learned Smokey's message about forest fire prevention.

Thirty years ago, artist Chuck Kuderna painted Smokey for the annual advertising campaign. His rendition of the fire prevention bear was very much like the earlier ones. Yet his Smokey was especially likable, with a very warm appeal. Since 1965, it has been a guide for what the Smokey Bear symbol should look like.

Here is Smokey Bear
as Chuck Kuderna painted him for the
1965 advertising poster.

In one of his early posters, Smokey says a special thanks to those
who are careful when using the forest for hunting, fishing, and other sports.

The Live Bear

A very important part of the Smokey Bear story is about the live Smokey that lived at the National Zoo for many years.

In the spring of 1950, there was a terrible forest fire in Lincoln National Forest, New Mexico. After the fire was over, a badly burned bear cub was found clinging to a charred tree snag. He was rescued by fire fighters and taken to the nearest fire camp.

Game warden Ray Bell took the cub to a doctor in Santa Fe to have his burns treated. A few days later, Bell returned and took the cub home with him. There his wife Ruth nursed the little orphan back to health.

The burned cub is treated by Dr. E. J. Smith in Santa Fe.

Judy Bell helped her mother take care of the little Smokey.

The cub became great friends with four-year-old Judy Bell and the family's black cocker spaniel, Jet. But the cub's days at the Bell home would soon be past.

All over America, people heard the sad story of the little burned cub and his narrow escape from fire. Naturally, they started calling him "Smokey" after the popular forest fire prevention symbol.

Soon the state of New Mexico sent the cub to the National Zoo in Washington, D. C., as a "gift to the school children of America." His own special airplane took the cub to Washington.

Pilot Homer Pickens waits with Smokey beside the
Piper Cub plane that will take the cub to Washington, D. C.

The bear at the Zoo became a living legend. He was called "Smokey Bear" and had his own outdoor quarters with a wide glass front so his friends could see him close-up. In front of his enclosure, a display board with pictures told his story.

The live Smokey was a very popular resident at the Zoo. Millions of children, their parents, and other friends of Smokey followed a wooded path to the bear quarters to see him.

At the National Zoo, the cub Smokey grew into a handsome adult bear.

The living Smokey Bear remained at the Zoo until his death in 1976, of illness and old age. His body was returned to Capitan, New Mexico for burial. Capitan is known as "Smokey Bear's Home Town" because it is near where he was found.

In Capitan there is a small Smokey Bear State Park, where Smokey's grave is marked by a giant boulder. On it is a metal plaque with an inscription about Smokey.

The Park Visitor's Center has on display many pictures, posters, and other Smokey Bear things. Visitors can see a film that tells the story of the live bear.

The people of Capitan are very proud of Smokey Bear. Every July they have a big rodeo and celebration called the "Smokey Bear Stampede."

A very large statue of Smokey Bear stands inside the Visitor's Center at Smokey Bear State Park.

LEAVE CAMPFIRES COLD

SMOKEY

DROWN

STIR

FEEL

Help PREVENT FOREST FIRES!

One way that the U. S. Forest Service sends out Smokey Bear's message
is on coloring sheets for children.

Smokey Bear Still Going Strong

The story of the live bear who was rescued from a forest fire is so well-known that many people think he was the original Smokey Bear. But, as we know, the Smokey Bear advertising symbol was almost six years old when the burned cub came on the scene.

Year after year, even while there was a live Smokey at the Zoo, the advertising bear has steadily gone about his work of forest fire prevention. His popularity has grown so much that people all over the world recognize him. Most of them can repeat his best-known message: "Remember-- Only YOU can prevent forest fires!"

Smokey gets so much mail that, many years ago, he was given his very own zip code. His official address is:

Smokey Bear Headquarters
Washington, D. C. 20252

Here is a most appealing poster showing
Smokey's sadness over a wasted forest.
It is also one of the earliest posters using
his best-known message.

Smokey Cares About Trees

Just asking people to be careful with fire in the forest is not all that Smokey does. He urges us to think of every tree in the forest as something special, worthy of our care and appreciation.

Trees provide so many things we need. Even if we tried, we could not name them all.

It takes many, many trees to make a cool, shady forest or park where we can go for camping, or picnics, or just to hike or play.

Smokey reminds us that it took a long time for each tree in the forest to grow. Even very tiny trees can be five or six years old. And the tall trees of the forest can be five or six *hundred* years old!

It's more than a tree.
It's "Let's pretend."

How many tree-houses, forts, hideaways and castles can a tree be? Ask a kid.

Only you can prevent forest fires.

Part of an Advertising Council annual campaign, this may not seem to come from Smokey Bear. But look carefully and you find his image and fire prevention message.

BURNING TIME—ONE CARELESS MOMENT

Remember—only <u>YOU</u> can prevent forest fires!

Because he cares about the trees, Smokey Bear begs you to remember how much time and how many trees it takes to make a forest. Then remember how quickly a careless fire can burn it all down.

Not all fires are bad. Some fire is needed to preserve the natural environment of the forest. But there are plenty of fires caused by natural happenings, such as lightning. Also, controlled burning is good, when done by foresters who know how and when it is safe. We all know that Smokey is not trying to stop natural fires or controlled burning. Yet he is trying to prevent forest fires caused by careless people who do not follow fire safety rules, or by people who accidentally set off a fire.

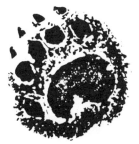

Trash Fires

You may think it is strange to include trash fires when we are talking about Smokey Bear. Yet trash fires are a very serious problem. Smokey knows that.

Many people live in or near forests. Often they may want to build fires to burn trash. That is all right if it is done carefully, so that the fire does not spread out of control.

A runaway fire is not only a danger to homes. It can reach a wooded area and cause a forest fire. Then it gets into Smokey Bear territory. No wonder he warns people to be careful with trash fires!

By 1960, Smokey included trash burning in his fire warnings.

Smokey and the Forest Creatures

Smokey Bear could not care so much for the trees without also caring for the forest creatures who live among them. Many posters show him with these animal friends.

Sometimes the animals are clustered about Smokey. At other times, the animals themselves remind people to be careful.

Most people like these pictures. It strikes a warm spot in your heart to see the trusting eyes of an animal looking directly at you from a poster.

Please...be careful!
PREVENT FOREST FIRES!

- BREAK YOUR MATCHES
- CRUSH YOUR SMOKES
- DROWN YOUR CAMPFIRES
- BE CAREFUL WITH ANY FIRE!

Thanks, SMOKEY

Although Smokey is not a symbol for wildlife conservation, animals and birds have been an important part of his fire prevention advertising from the very beginning. You could hardly be concerned about a burning forest, and not worry about what happens to its wild residents.

Two of Smokey's forest friends peep over his advertising sign.

...and please make people careful, amen

Some of the fire prevention posters have "woods fires" instead of "forest fires", especially in southern states.

Remember - Only you can PREVENT WOODS FIRES!

While his friends stand close by, Smokey prays that people will be careful with fire.

Smokey Bear cares about
the wild creatures of the forests.
He knows they suffer during
forest fires.

Forest fires sometimes burn birds' nests and kill
baby birds.

If forest fires burn their homes, animals have to find other places to live.

How life begins in the forest.

American Robin

Northern Red Oak

Spotted Frog

Beaver

Northern Scarlet Snake

Red Fox

Nursery Web Spider

Barn Owl

Mule Deer

Ponderosa Pine

How it ends.

One match.
That's all it takes to destroy a forest and every creature, great and small, who lives there.
So it's especially important to be careful with fire when you're in the forest.
Always make sure your campfire is out cold before you leave it. If you see someone being careless with fire, call an adult. And never, ever play with matches.
Remember, only you can prevent forest fires.

SMOKEY

Forest creatures appear for Smokey on a 1990 advertising poster.

Smokey and the Cubs

Two special forest creatures that sometimes help Smokey Bear are two busy little bears. Many people think they are his own cubs. But they are not. They are just his good friends and helpers.

The cubs were first included in Smokey pictures many years ago. They were very clever, and became popular. So they have been with him ever since.

Although Smokey still appears alone most of the time, you can surely expect to see his little helpers with him very often. You never know what they will be doing. Part of the time you may see them busy at something, with Smokey nowhere in sight.

It's no secret that
these cubs
never play with
matches. They
also don't like
it when people
discard live cigarettes
in the forest,
or go away and
leave a campfire without drowning it.

When Smokey Was Thirty

In 1974, when Smokey was thirty years old, **"THINK"** was used in the advertising campaign. There were five different messages. Each was printed under the huge word **"THINK."** The subject of each message stood in the middle of the word, where the **"I"** should be.

Three of the messages are shown here. Remember, they were printed over twenty years ago. But the things that Smokey Bear tells us mean as much today as they did in 1974.

In the thirty years that Smokey Bear has been telling us to be careful with fire, we've cut the number of forest fires we start in half.

But we still start over 100,000 careless fires every year.

Someday, one of two things will happen, and Smokey will stop reminding us to be careful: Either there won't be any more forest fires, or there won't be any more forests.

It's up to you.

Careless forest fires in America burn an average of sixteen trees every second.

They burn two million acres of valuable land every year.

They burn campsites. And vacation areas.

And homes.

And that's not all they burn.

So, please, think before you strike.

It's one thing to save a forest. But it's quite another to save a life.

Every year, every man, woman and child in the United States consumes the equivalent of a 100 foot tree—in lumber, paper products, and things we use every day. That's 200 million trees a year. And the demand is growing every day.

So, the next time you visit the forest, think about the 500 million precious trees we destroyed last year with careless fire. They take an extra minute to be careful.

The tree you save may be your own.

Smokey Says

In his long history, Smokey Bear has received help in many ways. One was a series of cartoons called "Smokey Says." They started in the South when the fire prevention symbol was very new.

The cartoons appeared in newspapers, once a week. Each one was very small, and fitted into a single newspaper column. Under the picture was a wise saying from Smokey.

Smokey Says:

AMERICA ..the Beautiful!

Keep it that way— Prevent forest fires!

Smokey Says:

"Just think – it will require HALF A CENTURY or more for Nature to restore this blackened waste!"

Help prevent forest fires! Save our forest resources!

Smokey Says:

PLEASE..PROTECT LITTLE TREES!

Prevent Forest Fires!

The "Smokey Says" cartoons originating in Atlanta, Georgia, were the idea of a Forest Service man, H. M. Sears. The cartoons were drawn by various artists. Harry Rossoll drew four cartoons a month for many years. Rudy Wendelin also drew some of them. The series began in 1947, and by 1951 were sent to newspapers throughout the United States. They continued until the mid-1970's.

Smokey Says:

PLEASE . . . Be Careful!

Smokey Says:

— they'll never learn until it's too late!

Smokey Says:

Preventing fire is
everybody's business!

Smokey Says:

Prevent forest wildfires!

Smokey Says:

Don't be the cause of a
forest fire!

Smokey's friends don't play with matches.

An intricate paper sculpture presents Smokey
and forest friends for a 1971 poster.

This 1989 poster shows that Smokey's message is so well known, only the first two words are needed to remind people to be careful. The poster was first used in 1985 and was so popular that it was re-issued for the time leading up to Smokey's 50th birthday.

Two chipmunks pause to study Smoky's sign.

"The" Bear

Smokey has appeared on television often in his long history. One of those times was an hour-long program in 1966, called "The Ballad of Smokey the Bear."

The show was very special because Smokey and his friends were produced in "Animagic." The characters were figures that were moved a little bit at a time to make the action for the film. It was very popular, and was shown many more times.

Smokey is shown here as he appeared in "The Ballad of Smokey the Bear."

You may have heard that Smokey Bear does not have "the" in the middle of his name. He does not. But people sometimes make mistakes and put a "the" in his name anyway. That happened when "The Ballad of Smokey the Bear" was written. The same thing happened a long time ago when a song was written, called "Smokey the Bear." That song is still a great favorite with children who like the fire prevention bear.

Sometimes Smokey Is Big

Smokey Bear often can be seen bigger than life-size, especially when he goes to a parade.

The Macy's Thanksgiving Day Parade in New York City had a Smokey Bear balloon that was 59 feet tall. It first appeared in the 1966 parade. About 40 million people saw it, either at the parade, or on television.

Big balloons like those used in parades usually last only about five years. But the Smokey balloon lasted longer. It was in the Macy's parade for five years. Then it was brought back a number of times in later years.

In celebration of Smokey's up-coming 50th birthday, Macy's used the balloon in their 1993 Thanksgiving Day Parade.

Smokey Bear also has been seen many times on floats in the Tournament of Roses Parade, held every New Year's Day in Pasadena, California.

Some giant figures of Smokey travel in a different way. North Carolina state foresters have a Smokey that is so big he must be transported lying down on a flat-bed truck. He was built in 1984, and goes all over North Carolina to fairs and other events. When standing up, he is 21 feet tall.

There are many oversize copies of Smokey that do not move at all. A 26-foot tall statue of the fire prevention bear has been standing in the city park of International Falls, Minnesota, since 1954.

The Smokey Bear balloon was so huge,
it took many strong hands to test it
for the Macy's Parade.

Of course, we have mentioned only a few giant figures of Smokey Bear. There are many more of them, in different places around the country. But they are all alike in one special way: each one is a great reminder to a lot of people that they should help prevent forest fires.

Smokey remembers to thank people
who heed his message.

A Law to Protect Smokey

When Smokey Bear was only seven years old, the U. S. Congress passed a law to protect him. He needed protection to keep his name and image from being used in the wrong way.

Anyone who wants to use Smokey's picture or name on something being made for sale must apply to the USFS for a license. When the license is granted, a royalty fee is paid to the CFFP Program. Every licensed product must have a forest fire prevention message.

You can go into many gift shops and other stores and see licensed Smokey Bear products. There are so many that we could not name them all. Even books about Smokey Bear need to be licensed.

The royalty money from licensees goes into a special account, and is used for forest fire prevention. So Smokey Bear, through the licensed products, helps to support his own program.

The law that protects Smokey was approved May 23, 1952, as Public Law 359 of the 82nd Congress. It was amended in 1974 as Public Law 93-318 of the 93rd Congress. It is better known as the "Smokey Bear Act."

Fire destroys <u>his</u> trees, too

REMEMBER — ONLY <u>YOU</u> CAN PREVENT FOREST FIRES!

Small trees are the forests of the future. When a forest fire destroys
even the seedlings, the whole forest has to start over again.

Children and Smokey

Children have always been very special to Smokey. They are his best supporters. They not only listen to what the fire prevention bear tells them. They also repeat his warnings to adults.

When Smokey Bear appears in person, it is most often at some place where there are many children. It makes quite an impression on students when a forest ranger comes to talk to them in their classroom and brings Smokey Bear with him. Smokey's message seems much more important when he's right in the same room looking at you!

Classrooms are not the only place where you can see Smokey in person. He goes many places. He is a frequent guest at state fairs and rodeos. He goes to many ball games, races, and other sporting events. Everywhere he goes, his message goes with him, in the form of Smokey Bear souvenirs and information.

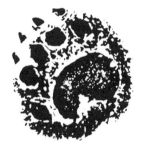

Of course you know that when Smokey appears in public and walks around among people, it's not really a bear. It's a person dressed up in costume. But that's the only way for the bear to "come alive" and visit his friends.

Even Smokey's warning sign is partly burned in this picture from a coloring sheet. Teachers and youth leaders can get coloring sheets and other items free from either U. S. Forest Service or State Forest Service offices.

It's fascinating to meet Smokey personally. There is nothing like looking up into the face of a six-foot-tall bear, to make you pay attention to his fire prevention message! Also, it is a lot of fun to say you actually saw Smokey Bear, and perhaps even touched his fur, or shook his hand.

Don't expect Smokey Bear to talk to you, though. The bear really is not supposed to speak. There is always someone with him to act as speaker for him.

There are specific rules about wearing the Smokey Bear costume. An officially approved costume should be used, and should be worn by a person in the Forest Service, or someone whom they authorize to wear it. Since the costume is big and visibility is poor, Smokey needs an assistant with him at all times, to guide him up and down steps, past any obstacles, and under low doorways, overhanging branches, overhead wires, and similar hazards. Since Smokey Bear isn't supposed to speak, the assistant also serves as Smokey's spokesperson.

Smokey visits in person with two of the many friends who came to his 50th Birthday celebration in Washington, D. C.

Junior Forest Rangers

One of the most successful parts of the Smokey Bear story has been the Junior Forest Ranger Program. It's very interesting how it got started.

It all began when Ideal Toys made the first Smokey Bear stuffed animal for sale in 1952. When the company applied for a license, it asked permission to include with each animal an application blank. A child could fill in the blank and send it to Smokey Bear Headquarters asking to become a Junior Forest Ranger.

The results were amazing. Three years later, there were a half-million Junior Forest Rangers. They were a powerful force behind Smokey's forest fire prevention program.

It was said that Junior Forest Rangers knew more about forest fire prevention than most adults. Their numbers continued to grow, until over five million youngsters had joined.

There is still a Junior Forest Ranger Program. Any child who wants to join can send in a personal written request to Smokey Bear Headquarters, Washington, D. C., 20252.

Smokey's Fiftieth Birthday

Most of us celebrate our birthdays on a single day. But Smokey Bear's fiftieth birthday was so important, the celebration began a whole year early!

From the summer of 1993, people all over the country were engaged in all sorts of activities to honor the fire prevention bear. The U. S. Forest Service issued a video presentation about Smokey Bear. Travelling museums showed interesting exhibits of Smokey Bear objects and information about his history. Many towns and cities staged Smokey Bear birthday events, months ahead of the actual date.

It's easy to understand why there was such a long birthday celebration for Smokey. The bear has so many friends all over America and in other countries as well, that it would impossible to celebrate his birthday in just *one day*.

Finally the real birthday did arrive. A big, day-long, outdoor event was held on the Ellipse in Washington, D. C., on August 9, 1994.

A 21-foot tall Smokey Bear from North Carolina towers above the crowd at Smokey's birthday celebration in Washington. The head, arm. and mouth of the figure moved.

There were fun things to do, lots of music, many awards, interesting exhibits, and entertainment. Smokey Bear in costume, escorted by a forest ranger, wandered around in the crowd to visit with his friends. In the afternoon, people on the Ellipse in Washington saw Smokey Bear on live television, leading the parade down Main Street at Disney World. The crowd sang "Happy Birthday" to Smokey.

After the celebration was all over, friends said good-bye Then Smokey Bear was ready to put on his campaign hat, pick up his shovel, and start to work on the *next* fifty years.

REMEMBER...

SMOKEY HAS FOR FIFTY YEARS

16USC580

Smokey Bear's 50th Anniversary Commemorative Logo.

What Does Smokey Stand For?

We all know that Smokey is the *forest fire* prevention bear. That is still the main thing he is concerned about.

Yet, many people now think of Smokey as the protector of all wild areas that might be in danger if people cause careless fires. If we think of him in that way, what does Smokey Bear stand for?

He stands for giant redwoods and little dogwoods. He stands for tall trees like palms and pines, for spreading shade trees like oaks and maples. He even stands for unique trees like those that abound in Joshua Tree Forest in Arizona. He stands for forest growth under the trees, and for growth in areas where there are no trees. He stands for vast prairies that wildfires can destroy. Wherever there is natural growth in danger from careless human-caused fire, Smokey takes his stand.

It is comforting to think of Smokey as against all wildfires. But don't forget that his best-known message is still: REMEMBER - Only YOU can prevent forest fires!

Glossary

conservation: protecting natural resources, such as forests, water, and animals.

controlled burning: fire set by authorized persons at safe times, to help the environment.

environment: the area and things all around us.

quizzical: questioning.

sabotage: bad acts by enemy agents, meant to hurt a country's production or business during wartime.

unique: rare or unusual; unlike any other.

wildfire: fire that spreads rapidly and is hard to put out.

Index

(Page numbers printed in **bold** type have pictures relating to the subject.)

A, B, C's 11
Advertising symbol 2, 3, 6.

"Ballad of Smokey the Bear" **45**.
Bambi **3**.
Burned forest **8, 24, 50**.

Capitan 21, 14.
CFFP Program 4.
Children **9**, 51.
Commemorative stamp **14**.
Controlled burning 27.
Cubs **37**.

Fiftieth Birthday Celebration **55-56**.
Fiftieth Birthday Logo **56**
Fiftieth Birthday Program Poster **12**.
Foreign language poster **4**.
Forest creatures **10, 29, 32 - 34, 42**.
Free educational materials **52**.

Junior Forest Rangers **54**.

Kuderna, Chuck **15**.

Live Smokey **17 - 29**.

Macy's Parade balloon 46, **47**.
Matches **34**.

"Only YOU" poster **43**.

Paper sculpture **42**.
Praying Smokey **31**.

Rossoll, Harry **40**.
Smokey and Cubs **35-36**.
Smokey Bear Law 49.
Smokey Says **40-41**.
Smokey costume 51, **53**, 56.
Smokey Bear State Park **21**.
Smokey figure, North Carolina 46, **55**.
Smokey statue, International Falls 46.
Staehle, Albert **5**, 6, **17**.

"Thanks" posters **16, 48, 61**.
"The" bear 45.
"THINK" posters **38-39**.
Tournament of Roses Parade 46.
Trash fires **28**.
Trees **25-27, 57**.

USDA 4.
USFS 4.

Wartime Advertising Council 4.
Wendelin, Rudy **13-14, 40**.
World War II 2.

Zip code 23.
Zoo 19, **20**.

Acknowledgments

Illustrations:

Page 14, Commemorative Stamp, *Courtesy of U. S. Postal Service.*

Pages 21, 55, 57, Photographs, *by Ellen E. Morrison.*

Page 53, Photograph, *by James R. Morrison.*

All other illustrations, *Courtesy of U.S. Department of Agriculture, Forest Service.*

Sincere appreciation is expressed
to Elsie Cunningham for
giving so generously of her time in helping
me to compile the material for this book.

-- *Ellen Earnhardt Morrison*

About the Author:

*Ellen Earnhardt Morrison was a free-lance contributor to juvenile periodicals while she was raising her four children. Now she specializes in writing history. She is author of the popular adult reference text **Guardian of the Forest: A History of the Smokey Bear Program.** She and her husband live in Alexandria, Virginia.*